I0844078

Jesus and the Internet of Things

Connectedness in a World of Devices

Table of Contents

Chapter 1. Introduction

Dive into an enlightening exploration of spirituality and tech development with our Special Report: "Jesus and the Internet of Things: Connectedness in a World of Devices." This exceptional study leaps into the intersection of theology and emerging technology, examining how the profound principles embodied by Jesus Christ resonate within our increasingly interconnected world of smart devices. With a lively blend of thought-provoking insights and heartening observations, this report is a captivating guide for anyone seeking to understand the spiritual dimensions of our modern digital landscape. Find in these pages a refreshing perspective that will not only enrich your knowledge base, but also inspire you to embrace technology with renewed consciousness and ethical grounding. Isn't it time to let the wisdom of the ages illuminate our digital future? Secure your copy today!

Chapter 2. Exploring the Intersections: Spirituality and Technology

Since the dawn of human history, religion and technology have intertwined, each shedding light on the other. Early civilizations saw the world imbued with spirit, forming mythology around natural occurrences that we now explain through science and technology. Likewise, as our technologies evolve, they influence our metaphysical beliefs, expanding our perspective on the divine. From the abacus to the Internet of Things, our tools shape our understanding of ourselves, our universe, and our place in it.

2.1. The Historical Synergy Between Spirituality and Technology

Central to understanding the overlap between spirituality and technology is recognizing their shared history. Civilizations have always used their contemporary technologies to interact with and express their spiritual beliefs. In ancient times, people carved deities into stone, built grand temples with primitive tools, and tracked the stars using primitive devices. As technology improved, religious expression evolved correspondingly: from handwritten manuscripts to the printed Bible, to spiritual radio broadcasts and televangelist TV shows.

Technology and spirituality often developed in close proximity. For instance, Gutenberg's printing press was instrumental in the Protestant Reformation, allowing for the mass production of Bibles and spreading Protestant beliefs across Europe. Today, modern technology like the Internet and the Internet of Things (IoT) promise a similar transformative impact on spirituality. However, the intersection is no longer one-directional; it has dynamically evolved into a reciprocal relationship where spirituality influences technology and vice versa.

2.2. The Influence of Jesus's Teachings on the Ethical Framework of Technology

Perhaps no figure has had as significant an influence on the ethical framework surrounding technology as Jesus Christ. His teachings on humility, equality, and respect for the dignity of all people provide guiding principles for responsible technology use. These notions of kindness, altruism, and care for others reflect in the design and operation of technology.

Technology often mirrors the nature of its creators, those who design and implement it. Therefore, people inspired by the ethical values of Jesus tend to create technology that encapsulates those principles. For instance, assistive technology for people with disabilities, or platforms that promote equity and inclusivity, exemplify love and compassion introduced by Jesus.

Similarly, the essence of 'connectedness' inherent in the IoT is a mirror of the spiritual connectivity preached by Jesus. The interconnection between devices serves as a tangible metaphor for the interconnectedness of humanity. By embracing the IoT, we echo Jesus's teachings about the importance of unity and interconnectivity.

2.3. Spirituality in a Hyper-Connected World

The IoT, which enables seamless communication between devices, is creating a world that's interconnected like never before. This interconnectedness offers intriguing spiritual implications that resonate with Jesus's teachings.

Jesus taught that every person has a unique, intrinsic worth as part of a greater whole. In the IoT, each device, regardless of its function or value, contributes to the overall network. Think of fitness trackers, smart home security systems, automated agricultural devices - each unique in function, yet all part of the IoT ecosystem. The beauty of this grand interconnection reflects the unity amid diversity preached by Jesus.

2.4. Guiding the Ethical Use of Technology with Spirituality

However, there are challenges and responsibilities that come with this unprecedented interconnectedness. These reflect in ethical dilemmas like privacy breaches, data mismanagement, and potential misuse of technology. Just as Jesus guided humanity centuries ago, we need similar guidance in addressing contemporary challenges.

Such guidance could be derived from the teachings of Jesus. His emphasis on love, respect for dialogue, and consent offers potential solutions. This approach could help establish ethics around asking permission before collecting data, prioritizing transparency with users about how their data is being used, and respecting digital rights.

2.5. Cultivating Conscious Connectivity

Through conscious connectivity we can navigate the digital landscape with awareness, equipping ourselves to make ethical choices that honor our shared values. If we approach technology with the humility and thoughtfulness inspired by Jesus, we begin to see not only the utility in our devices but also their potential for fostering greater empathy, understanding, and unity.

In conclusion, the intersection of spirituality and technology is not a new phenomenon. However, it's an area continually evolving in importance and complexity, urging us to not only use our technical skills but also invoke our spiritual abilities. As we look forward to a world increasingly dominated by technology, the teachings of Jesus offer an ethical grounding upon which to base our digital future. Embracing this perspective ensures a harmonious symphony between spirituality and technology, creating a more compassionate and connected world.

Chapter 3. Jesus' Teachings in a Digital Age: A New Interpretation

In our journey to explore the amalgamation of spirituality and technology, we first turn towards some of the core teachings of Jesus and their relevance in the digital age we inhabit.

3.1. Embracing the Connected World: Love thy Neighbour

The Biblical command to "love thy neighbour as thyself" presents us a golden rule that finds new interpretations in an interconnected digital world. Today, our interactions aren't just limited to our physical neighbours, but extend across countries and continents. Love, in a digital context, can be defined as respect, empathy, and understanding for others, their viewpoints, and their privacy. In the age of social media, this teaching gives us a manual on how to behave ethically and fairly online.

Before posting or sharing online, one might consider if their actions align with this principle. Does the content highlight respect and empathy, or does it sow chaos and negativity? Understanding that everyone connected with us through the internet is also our neighbour encourages a more compassionate online behaviour.

3.2. Digitization of Loaves & Fishes: Technology as a Tool

The miracle of the loaves and fishes, where Jesus fed thousands with a mere five loaves and two fish, signifies the powerful potential of small beginnings and the essence of sharing. We can view technology as a digital form of the loaves and fishes. Despite originating from small beginnings, it has the potential to reach billions of lives influencing education, healthcare, and fundamental human rights.

Digital tools can democratize access to knowledge, revolutionize healthcare, and empower individuals. Each innovative device, application, or platform has the potential to spread goodness around the globe, much like the loaves and fish. We must remember to use technology ethically, honing its power to create and share rather than hoard resources or deepen socio-economic divides.

3.3. Spaces of Sermon – Virtual Gathering and Community

One of Jesus's acts that made lasting impressions was his ability to gather people and share sermons. In today's digital era, this very act is repeated through webinars, online meetings, and posts shared across social platforms. The pandemic necessitated virtual congregations where the gospel was shared on digital platforms, bridging the gap between physical distancing and spiritual connectedness.

However, concerns such as 'trolling' and 'doxxing' present significant issues in these virtual spaces, necessitating the guiding light of teachings such as Jesus's adage to "treat others as you would like to be treated." By creating safe, inclusive, and respectful spaces, we can emulate the community spirit present during Jesus's sermons.

3.4. Ethical Citizenship: Do Not Cast the First Stone

The act of passing judgement on others has amplified in the digital age. Slander, gossip, and public shaming find new heights on platforms with worldwide reach. Jesus' solution to this age-old problem was expressed in his admonition: "He that is without sin among you, let him first cast a stone at her."

Translating this to our digital world, we note the importance of digital kindness. Avoiding online vilification and checking the spread of harmful content align directly with Jesus's lesson. Practice awareness of the fact that all individuals have their missteps and faults, which can help foster a more compassionate and caring digital community.

3.5. The Final Judgement – Digital Legacy

The concept of the final judgement — the last day where every individual will face their deeds — has a robust analogy in the digital realm. Every action on the internet leaves a digital footprint, creating a lasting legacy which may be a source of joy or regret in the future.

By considering future judgment, users might navigate their online actions more consciously. Whether writing a social media post, passing a comment, or sending a direct message, awareness of the permanence of digital actions can facilitate more mindful online interactions.

In essence, the teachings of Jesus can offer profound guidance on navigating the digital landscape. Central to these teachings are empathy, kindness, and love for one's neighbor, whether physical or digital. Interpreted anew for this digital age, they can function as a moral compass, helping individuals to engage effectively, ethically, and consciously with the wonders of the interconnected world. The wisdom of the ages thus illuminates the path towards a conscious digital future.

Chapter 4. Connectedness and Community: IoT and the Church

Technology has often been perceived as a bane rather than a boon to community kinship. Yet, as we delve deeper into the study of the Internet of Things (IoT) in relation to the Church, and more broadly, spirituality, a new perspective unfolds. This chapter attempts to unravel the potential of IoT in fostering a heightened sense of connectedness and community within the framework of Christian theology, all the while maintaining the essence of Jesus's teachings.

4.1. On Linking IoT and the Church: A Possibility?

Most people, when they think of IoT, envision smart homes, self-driving cars, or complex industrial systems. However, IoT's potential extends far beyond these material applications. The primary concept behind the Internet of Things - the idea of interconnectedness and communication between devices - fiercely resonates with the idea of a spiritual community.

Imagine a system where every believer, connected via a network, can interact with one another and the Church. This is not about bringings gadgets into the church, but enhancing the church's role as a spiritual and social focal point. In this way, IoT could potentially serve as a digital augmentation of fellowship, making the Church's teachings on unity, participation, and love more accessible and tangible.

4.2. The IoT-infused Worship: A Radical Shift

As we move further into the elaborate network of connected devices that IoT promises, the idea of IoT-infused worship is worth considering. From shared online sermons to virtual prayer meetings, IoT offers opportunities to maintain and enhance live worship services, even in the face of physical or geographical constraints.

Imagine a network of smart devices, streaming the sermon live for all congregants, near and far. Or consider a prayer meeting, held via the network, generating a constellation of faith connections and a deeper sense of unity. Anyone, devoid of geographical location, could participate in the sacred rituals, thus breaking down the barriers of isolation.

The possibilities, of course, come with responsibilities: ensuring the sacredness of rituals, respecting privacy, and upholding the sanctity of worship. Yet, we shouldn't discard the potential because of the challenge. On the contrary, these are opportunities to weave the essence of Jesus's teachings into our digital interactions.

4.3. IoT, Remoulding Pastoral Care

One of the central tenets of the Christian faith is to "love thy neighbor." In the past, this has been physically manifested by providing support and care within one's local community. Now, IoT brings a new dimension to pastoral care.

IoT can transform pastoral care from a local activity to a global one. Smart devices can be programmed to send reminders of prayer timings, Bible verses, or upcoming Church events. Health-monitoring wearables can notify groups of any health anomalies amongst the congregation, prompting quick community-led assistance where required. Indeed, IoT demonstrates the potential to transform the

Church's role in maintaining spiritual and social welfare among its followers.

4.4. Ethical Implications: A Crucial Consideration

While it is tempting to embrace IoT's potential without reservation, it is critical to examine the ethical implications of such precipitous adoption. Privacy is front and center in this discussion. Maintaining the sanctity of personal information amidst this interconnected orchestra of devices is paramount.

The principle of "loving thy neighbor" should extend to respecting one's privacy and ensuring the safe handling of personal information. Thus, information privacy should be an integral part of the Church's adoption of IoT. Transparent policies and safeguards will indeed be an essential component of this new age interconnectedness.

4.5. The IoT Vision: A Path Forward

At this juncture, the vision of IoT fostering a globally connected Church may seem distant, even utopian. However, this path forward hinges on our readiness to embrace this technology while adhering to the core spiritual principles.

As we navigate through this new digital landscape, let's recall the words of Jesus in the Gospel of Matthew, "For where two or three are gathered in my name, there am I among them." Whether these gatherings happen in a physical or a digital world, the promise remains the same.

The IoTC (the Internet of Things Church) can be perceived as the Church itself, transformed and optimized, through Jesus's teachings, to radiate a greater sense of community and connectedness. For those ready to navigate the challenges and harness the opportunities, this path shines with promise. Only through exploration and experience will we understand the profound impacts and truly tap the spiritual dimensions of our increasingly digital landscape.

In conclusion, while the intersection of theology and emerging technology is a complex terrain to maneuver, it also provides an exciting opportunity for enhancing connectedness and community within the Church, driven by the principles embodied by Jesus Christ. It is an exploration worth embarking upon; a journey where the wisdom of the ages can indeed illuminate our digital future.

Chapter 5. Walking the Path of Righteousness in a Smart World

One may wonder how spirituality, and specifically Christian ethics and teachings, can navigate through the ever-complex, dynamic digital landscape. An exploration of this blend prompts an inspiring dive into the essence of humanity in an increasingly automated and interconnected world.

5.1. Bridging the Digital and Spiritual Divide

Burgeoning technological developments in the field of the Internet of Things (IoT) have altered how we interact with the world. From smart home systems that automate daily routines to wearables that monitor health metrics, our lives reside in a tapestry woven with threads of technology.

Yet, as advanced as our gadgets become, human beings retain an intrinsic yearn for spiritual fulfillment and understanding, a yearn that Jesus sought to answer. His teachings, anchored on love, humility, and service, are timeless guideposts that can navigate us in this new digital landscape. They remind us of our purpose and the ultimate path of righteousness amidst the cacophony of advanced tech and data-driven decisions.

5.2. Tech Landscapes: Jesus' Ethos in Digital Interactions

Beyond the conventional applications of IoT lies a world of digital interactions that align surprisingly well with the principles that Jesus Christ espoused. The idea of interconnectedness at the heart of IoT resonates with his teachings of neighborly love, underscoring that just as devices in an IoT system work together for larger functional efficiency, humans must work in unity for the good of all.

Through the lens of Jesus' teachings, technology can foster an international 'neighborhood' that is connected, collaborative, and collectively focused on the common good. It's a framework that extends beyond mere functionality, delving into promoting the values of kindness, empathy, and mutual respect.

When viewed this way, walking the path of righteousness in a smart, digital world doesn't seem all that daunting.

5.3. Righteousness Defined Through Tech Behavior

What would being righteous in a world of smart devices look like? The essence of righteousness as taught by Jesus lies in maintaining an upright moral behavior and maintaining justice for all. In the digital sphere, this can translate to respectful online interaction, responsible sharing and consumption of digital content, and defending the digital rights of others, among others.

Even in designing and developing technology, the principles of righteousness can govern decisions. Ethical tech development moves beyond ROI and customer value; it takes into account the larger impact of a product or service on society and the environment. It considers data privacy concerns and the potential of tech abuse before it even arises.

5.4. Maintaining Humility in the Face of Advanced Tech

Some people may be captivated by the sophistication of cutting-edge technologies and consider them superior to all things before. However, the teaching of Jesus implies that humility is a virtue that should envelope our perspective on IoT advancements.

This involves acknowledging that despite the power and efficiency brought by these systems, technology is, at its core, a tool. It is not an end unto itself but a means that can be wielded for good or evil. Embracing this mindset compels us to stay observant and responsible, warding off the complacency that can result from overdependence or infatuation with technology.

5.5. Kneading Love into IoT: Service Through Technology

Jesus emphasized service to others as a primary expression of love. In the context of IoT, 'service' may translate into creating systems that are inclusive, accessible, and socio-economically considerate.

Accessibility in the IoT world suggests designing devices and software interfaces keeping in mind the varying abilities of users. Features like voice commands, simplified user interfaces, and affordable models can make technology a beneficial tool rather than a privilege of the few. Similarly, socio-economic consideration involves ensuring that technological advancements don't solely cater to high-end markets but reach across different economic strata.

5.6. Conclusion

In balancing the spiritual principles embodied by Jesus Christ with the prowess of technology, we find a path of righteousness that is tremendously applicable to our current digital landscape. These timeless insights and ethical guideposts allow us to navigate the digital world responsibly and humanely.

From advancing the principles of love and unity through interconnectedness, to upholding righteous behaviors in the digital sphere, to maintaining humility amidst sophisticated tech, and ultimately expressing love through valuable and inclusive technological service - this blend of spirituality and technology offers a roadmap to help light our path in the ever-evolving smart world.

As we continue to engage with technology in our day-to-day lives, it's key that we turn inward, drawing from the depths of our shared values and spiritual ethos to ensure that technology serves us and not the other way around. Remember, technology is as benevolent or destructive as the hands that steer it - the power to gear it towards a path of righteousness is in ours.

Chapter 6. Prayer in a Pulse: Spirituality in the Wireless Age

As we plunge hastily into the future where the tangible becomes intangible, yet somehow manages to hold increasingly greater significance in our day-to-day lives, we find ourselves standing at a unique junction. This intersection, where technology touches and engulfs every aspect of our existence, including our spiritual relationships and practices, forms the foundation of our discourse.

6.1. Discovery and Evolution of Prayer

Where, in this evolving world, does prayer fit in? Prayer, at its most essential, is an intrinsic human response to the vastness, intricacy, and mystery of life. It is the cry of a child seeking comfort, the joyful laughter ringing out in moments of sheer delight, the poignant sigh of a lonely heart. For centuries, these personal and communal conversations with divinity have thrived separately from technological progression. But modernity has curated a delicate bridge that links faith with gadgets – allowing computer chips and digital circuits to carry human aspirations heavenwards.

6.2. Digital Devotion: Apps and Platforms

The surge in faith-based apps like Pray.com, Echo Prayer, and Abide, is a clear testament to this blended world of spirituality and technology. These platforms serve as digital sanctuaries, allowing followers to engage in communal prayer and spiritual exercises at any time, and from any location. Thus, the confining parameters of conventional religious practice have ceded to the liberating, ubiquitous nature of the wireless age.

Barriers of availability, distance, and even disillusionment with institutionalized religion, often omnipresent with traditional methods, have been torn down. The transitional shift from physical to digital has not diluted the essence of prayer, but instead afforded greater accessibility, facilitating a more intimate and omnipresent interaction with the divine.

6.3. The Constancy of Connectivity and the Divine

But it's not only prayer that has transitioned into the digital realm. Scripture too, once bound to scrolls and print, now resides effervescently in the cloud. YouVersion, for instance, has revolutionized Bible readiness. With its free-to-download model, it caters to a growing demographic of digital-native worshippers who seek on-demand access to affirming wisdom and inspirational teachings. This demonstrates how technologies, like the Bible app, can actually increase engagement with religious texts, making it a handy tool for individuals seeking a deeper connection with their faith.

6.4. A New Generation of Devotees

The implications of digitizing scripture may seem superficial to some; yet they signify a broader shift in religious engagement among the youth. Traditional ceremonies and practices often fail to appeal to the younger generation's evolving mindsets, who may view them as outdated or out of touch with modern realities. However, digitization provides an attractive portal to access these ritualistic practices, spinning akin to the language they understand and the medium they consume. It has, therefore, widened the scope for involvement and fostered a renewed interest in religion.

6.5. The Challenges Ahead: Ethical Implications

However, shrouding the horizon, are the ethical implications that arise with the amalgamation of religion and technology. Issues such as data privacy, monetization of devotional activities, and the risk of diluting or distorting religious messaging due to the mass-market appeal. Striking the right balance is critical, the essence of prayer and devotion must not be lost amidst pixels and profit margins. The key is integrating technology in such a way that it complements and propagates our spiritual journeys, instead of compromising them.

6.6. The Interface of IoT and Spirituality

And then we come to the nascent stage of the Internet of Things (IoT), a realm where everyday objects are connected to the internet, gathering, processing, and exchanging data. Devices like Amazon's Alexa or smart watches are, quite literally, putting prayer in a pulse. We're only beginning to scratch the surface of what this might mean for the spiritual health and wellbeing of mankind. The potential application of IoT in breaking down barriers to entry, deepening engagement, and accelerating the growth of collective consciousness is vast. It represents a whole new frontier where the lines between the material and spiritual worlds might thin further.

6.7. Man-Machine and Divinity

The symbiosis of faith and technology is a dynamic phenomenon that we are barely beginning to grasp. It is the shining reflection of mankind's quest for integrated living. It's not about replacing traditional spirituality with technology; rather it's the exploration of new mediums to channel our prayer, devotion, and spiritual companionship. The critical challenge is to ensure that in embracing this technological dawn, we retain the sanctity and integrity of the spiritual practice, all the while embracing the tremendous opportunities for connectivity and collective growth that it affords.

In this rapidly evolving narrative of spirituality in the wireless age, the words of Christ resonate: "Love the Lord your God with all your heart and with all your soul and with all your mind." Perhaps in our context, we could consider the added dimension of loving God with all our network connections and all our smart devices, fervently embracing the richness of spiritual connectedness that our digital future offers. It's up to us to determine whether our future will be one of separation and disarray, or a fertile ground of inclusivity, enlightenment, and shared spiritual awakening derived from this boundless connection. In end, one thing is certain: God remains in our midst, constantly buzzing, just like the technology that surrounds us.

Chapter 7. Miracles Reimagined: The Divine Power of Technology

In the New Testament, Jesus performs various miracles—turning water into wine, healing the sick, feeding five thousand people from five loaves of bread and two fish, and even bringing the dead back to life. Today, we see an entirely different landscape, one filled with the noise of ones and zeros, laced with intricate patterns of technology – a world where miracles take on a whole new dimension.

7.1. The Healing Touch of Technology

Consider the remarkable advancements in the medical field. With the advent of technologies like 3D printing, bio-printing, and robotics, we are witnessing something akin to miracles. Doctors can now create prosthetics tailored to an individual's exact bodily measurements, making them more efficient and comfortable than ever before. We can generate human body parts, regrow cells, and even engineer human tissues in laboratories. These medical prosthetics and transplantations are reminiscent of Jesus's healing miracles, restoring the livelihoods of those who may have lost hope. Hence, while the method is different, the results mirror those of Christ's miracles—the restoration of health, happiness, and life.

Casting our eyes to the miraculous power of Christ in resurrecting the dead, we find analogies lurking in the realm of artificial intelligence and machine learning. Pioneering technologies such as predictive analysis and preventive health monitors have potentially life-saving applications. They can pre-empt diseases and complications, thereby averting mortal danger—the precursor to resurrection.

7.2. Refreshing Lives: The Miracle of Transformation

Change was a cornerstone of Jesus's miracles. Water became wine, a few loaves and fishes expanded into a meal for thousands. Today, the Internet of Things (IoT) empowers us to enact significant changes in our world. We can optimise water usage in agriculture with smart irrigation systems, reducing waste, and improving crop yield. IoT functions as our small basket of loaves and fishes able to feed an expanding global population. We transform data into actionable intelligence that makes our lives healthier, safer, and more organized.

Providing potable water to communities in need, especially in water-scarce regions, is another tangible miracle technology has abetted. Novel water purifying technologies, efficient desalination methods, and intelligent distribution networks are turning unsafe or brackish sources into life-saving freshwater.

7.3. The Miracle of Connection

Jesus's ministry was more than just physical miracles—it was about building connections and spreading love. His miracles were a bridge connecting people with God, highlighting the divine omnipresence. Today, technology encapsulates this connection aspect through the vast, intricate web referred to as the Internet.

With the Internet, we are more connected than ever before. Social media allows us to engage with friends and family from any corner of the globe with just a click. The Internet has revolutionized charity, enabling generous individuals to instantly donate to causes worldwide, often directly impacting lives.

Moreover, the Internet has made knowledge easily accessible, democratising education. Online courses and digital platforms have opened gates of wisdom for all, not unlike the enlightening teachings Jesus spread during his life.

7.4. Concluding Thoughts: The Godliness within Technology

While it may seem strange to draw parallels between Jesus's miracles and modern technological innovations, these comparisons illustrate how our present-day marvels align themselves with humanity's ancient spiritual aspirations. It demonstrates that while the form changes, the essence remains the same—making lives better.

Just as Jesus encouraged us to reach deeper into our humanity and compassion, technology urges us to innovate ethically and judiciously, leveraging the interconnectedness of the IoT construct to promote social equality, justice, and love. This awareness brings a higher dimension to technology, which, like spirituality, serves its highest purpose when aimed at the greater good.

As the world navigates through the ever-evolving landscape of AI, IoT, and automation, this understanding brings solace and hope. In the depths of algorithms and smart devices, we can find ourselves converging towards the principles Jesus embodied—love, charity, kindness, and connection. Technological advancements, when used wisely, yield modern-day miracles.

By perceiving the divine in technology, we understand how intertwined our spiritual and digital dimensions are. Indeed, the miracles we see today are not in conflict with the teachings of Jesus. Instead, they are a reimagining — a modern manifestation of the divine power that encourages us to be the best versions of ourselves in a rapidly changing world. It is about time we embrace this interconnected, miracle-filled digital journey with wonder, gratitude, and a renewed sense of responsibility.

Chapter 8. Serving Others in the Internet Age: Virtual Altruism

In the age of connectivity, where every individual with internet access can interact with each other regardless of geographical boundaries, serving others has taken on a more comprehensive scope. Emotional bonding, which used to be limited to physical interactions and geographic proximity, is now proliferating on various digital platforms, creating fertile soil for acts of selfless assistance and the sprouting of a new kind of altruism: Virtual Altruism.

8.1. The Emergence of Virtual Altruism: A New Landscape for Compassion

Virtual altruism is a product of the increasingly advanced technological milieu. It is the act of selflessly helping others on internet platforms without expecting anything in return. This radical manifestation of altruism can be seen when netizens unite to support a cause, donate to charities, or help those in need. The representation of Jesus's teachings in the digital era, virtual altruism, can be perceived through the socio-technical lens. Jesus taught us to "love thy neighbor," and in an internet world without fences, everyone can potentially be our neighbors.

Digital networks have become a powerful tool enabling individuals to reach across borders, cultures, and societies to offer support and solidarity. The internet's form—a limitless platform—allows for collective participation and shared responses, thereby magnifying the impact of such humanitarian actions. Virtual connections are replacing isolation with mutual support and solidarity, echoing Jesus's doctrine of love and camaraderie, and laying the groundwork for serving others in the digital age.

8.2. Digital Platforms as Catalysts of Change: Utilizing Social Media for Good

When we tie this to the concept of social media platforms, we understand that these platforms have become crucial intersection points for action, awareness, and aid in today's interconnected world. They enable individuals to communicate, engage, and act collectively. Such online actions reflect the embodiment of the Christan virtue of serving others and the Aristotelian principle of acting for the common good.

One striking example of how social media can be used as a tool for virtual altruism is the various crowdfunding campaigns organized to support people dealing with medical emergencies, educational requirements, or projects aimed at social upliftment. The internet community comes together, donating to causes they resonate with, and in doing so, exemplify the core Christian principle of offering help to strangers. This act resonates with Matthew 25:40, where Jesus says, "whatever you did for one of the least of these brothers and sisters of mine, you did for me."

8.3. Translating Empathy into Action: The Role of Digital Tithing

Despite the physical distance between individuals in the internet age, the sense of shared emotional experience is profoundly real—it evokes empathy and promotes action. This concept has given rise to the concept of digital tithing. The Christian practice of tithing, which involves giving a portion of one's income to the church or charity, has found a new expression in the digital era.

Digital tithing is a prime example of how traditional spiritual practices can adapt to technological advancements. It allows individuals to contribute financial resources electronically to causes that align with their beliefs and empathies. It is a modern take on a long-held practice, demonstrating that while the methods may change, the underlying principles of generosity and communal assistance remain.

8.4. Algorithms and Ethics: Fostering Transparent and Responsible Digital Altruism

However, the new landscape of altruism also presents new challenges. The internet has witnessed the manipulation of sentiment and the misuse of platforms intended for good. Thus, a careful approach to digital altruism is quintessential, guided by the ethical compass of Jesus's teachings.

In a world where algorithms often determine what we see, transparency becomes crucial. Technology developers and platform administrators must ensure that they foster a culture that upholds the ethical prism of virtual altruism. This includes not allowing the commercialization of empathetic gestures, and ensuring that help reaches the intended recipients without unjust manipulation. Crossing this digital divide with a clear ethical consciousness is a crucial step towards authentic virtual altruism.

In conclusion, serving others in the internet age—virtual altruism—holds immense potential as a beacon of hope and solidarity, as long as it is grounded in honest, transparent, and ethical principles. An understanding, application, and appreciation of Jesus's teachings in our interconnected digital world can foster a global culture of support, empathy, and love—resonating the profound message of the greatest spiritual leader to the furthest corners of our digital universe.

Chapter 9. Privacy, Ethics and the IoT: Lessons from the Bible

In the epoch of technological revolution, where smart devices and interconnected technology or the 'Internet of Things' (IoT) is reforming the way we live, work, and interact, the significance of privacy and ethics is intensifying. With humanity standing on the precipice of a digital future, we delve into the teachings of the Bible - unmasking timeless lessons and wisdom that could shed light on the path to ethically-sound technological innovation.

9.1. The Biblical Perspective on Privacy

An examination of biblical content won't yield a direct set of rules pertaining to modern privacy concerns. However, if we look deeper, we can extract profound principles that bear relevance in any era. Scripture has always underscored the importance of respect for individuals and their dignity. A striking example is the Tenth Commandment, which bars coveting anything that belongs to your neighbor (Exodus 20:17). In essence, it cautions against violating the boundary around your neighbor's life and possessions.

Bringing this principle to our tech-driven society, respect for privacy becomes an indispensable ethical norm. Today, the 'neighbor' could be anyone linked to us through the sprawling web of the IoT. Each smart device collects, processes, and broadcasts personal data - effectively blurring the lines around individual privacy. In the light of this, respecting an individual's privacy should be paramount, guiding IoT's development and governance.

9.2. Ethics in a Connected World: Lessons from the Sermon on the Mount

The Sermon on the Mount, one of Jesus Christ's most well-known teachings, might seem far removed from the digital world, but it rather offers invaluable lessons on ethical comportment. The eight Beatitudes, in particular, serve as pivotal ethical cornerstones (Matthew 5:3–12). 'Blessed are the merciful,' could be interpreted as a call for empathy and understanding in our connected world. Applying mercy in cyberspace, we're inspired to build and use technology that cares for the wellbeing of users.

'Blessed are the pure in heart,' reminds IoT developers that motives matter. It suggests that while technological advancements might allure with potential gains, the intent should always remain pure - prioritizing benefit to humankind.

9.3. Data Stewardship: Parable of the Talents

The Parable of the Talents (Matthew 25:14-30) offers insights into responsibility, accountability, and good stewardship, which coalesce into one of the Bible's vital teachings on data ethics. In a world where data is the new currency, it's imperative to manage it with utmost responsibility. The parable teaches that we are entrusted stewards, not owners, of resources. Businesses, as custodians of data, should handle it responsibly, ensuring fair and transparent usage.

Moreover, the Bible encourages good stewardship by rewarding those who use their talents wisely. In similar fashion, good data stewardship generates trust, transparency, and loyalty; well-recognized assets in our digital age.

9.4. Love your Neighbor as Yourself: Forming an Ethical IoT

As we steer through the tide of technology, the biblical commandment, 'Love your Neighbor as Yourself' stands unswerving. This commandment encapsulates the essence of ethical relationships. In the context of IoT, this can be interpreted as promoting interconnected devices that respect, protect, and nurture towards all users.

IoT developers need to incorporate ethical considerations right from the ideational phase, considering how data can be used, misused, and protected. Primarily, it means designing technology that respects user rights, ensures security, and negates discrimination.

Nurturing means developing tech that takes a user-centric approach, enhances lives, and nurtures human dignity. This approach ties back to the principle of beneficence, ensuring that technological endeavors aim to do good - a principle deeply embedded in Biblical teachings.

The intersection of spirituality and technology is a compelling sphere, hinged on shared principles that uphold dignity, promote respect, and strive for a goodwill-centered society. The Bible, through its timeless wisdom, ushers us towards an ethical digital future - one that reveres privacy, worships transparent stewardship, upholds virtuous intent, and always aims to do good. It reinforces the idea that technology should not merely serve humanity, but also reflect the basic norms and values that bind us together as a species.

In conclusion, the principles extrapolated from the Bible serve as guiding posts in the digital fog, enabling us to navigate the unchartered territories of IoT ethically and responsibly. The need of the hour is ethical awakening, ushering an era where technological evolution is harmonized with the principles of love, respect, and stewardship - the beating heart of all biblical teachings.

Chapter 10. Resurrection and Revival: Applying Wisdom to Failing Systems

In a world where systems and technologies are under constant challenge of obsolescence, it becomes imperative to reflect on the wisdom from our spiritual traditions to guide our path forward. Drawing inspiration from the story of resurrection—of revival from the seeming end—we articulate the possibilities that lay in the reinvention of our failing systems, through the lens of wisdom, learning, and interconnectedness.

10.1. Revival: Finding inspiration in adversity

Taking cues from the resurrection narrative, the first concept we address is revival. As Jesus triumphed over death, ushering in a new era of faith and hope, we must see an opportunity for revitalization amidst the seemingly defunct or failing systems of our technological world. Rather than clinging to the comfort of the familiar, we can recognize the need for disruption as a preparatory step for revival.

Consider, for example, the systems that once relied on fossil fuels. As the environmental consequences of these choices begin to breathe down our necks, instead of viewing the situation as a demise, we are championed to see it as the advent of a resurrection. This perspective shift paves the way for renewable energy solutions, reshaping the mosaic of our technology-centered lifestyles.

10.2. Resurrecting Systems: Wisdom over obsolescence

The concept of obsolescence lies at the heart of technology. The drive to continuously innovate and improve often leaves older systems or technologies behind, deemed irrelevant. Reviving these systems doesn't necessarily mean simply bringing back the old; rather, it implies learning from the wisdom they hold and applying that knowledge to shape the future.

Could we not find inspiration from the regeneration of a forest, for example, after a wildfire, and apply its principles to the recovery process of a cyber attack? The ashes of a system can indeed be the foundation for growth and renewal.

10.3. Lessons from Jesus: Embracing change, fostering transformation

The story of Jesus's resurrection also teaches an important lesson about the dialectics of change and transformation. There is a fundamental difference between change and transformation. Whereas change often implies simple layering or modification, transformation points towards a fundamental shift, an overhaul of the current state.

As we face significant global challenges—from climate change to socioeconomic disparities—it's apparent that mere changes will no longer suffice; a transformation is needed. Whether we're discussing green energy, universal basic income, or digital inclusivity, it isn't about a simple transition but about challenging the status quo and fostering deep-seated transformation.

10.4. Technology as a Tool: Applying wisdom to drive progress

Technology, in essence, is a tool—not a solution in itself. As we move forward, it's crucial to ensure we don't lose sight of this, pouring our collective wisdom into the conscious development of technologies that facilitate positive transformation. Whether it's artificial intelligence, Internet of Things, biotechnology, or any other frontier of innovation, using them judiciously to create sustainable, equitable, and inclusive solutions should be the goal.

10.5. Interconnectedness: Lessons from the web of life

In recognizing the interconnectedness of all things, underlying the narrative of resurrection and revival, we can draw valuable lessons for our technologically woven world. Internet of Things (IoT), as a metaphor, can serve to remind us that each device, and the individual it serves, is part of a wider fabric. Each thread plays an essential role in the resilience and health of the whole system.

As we apply this understanding to stimulate progress in our failing systems revisiting our concepts of success and progress might be essential. Is it the singular pursuit of speed, power, and efficiency? Or could it instead encompass harmony, inclusivity, and sustainability - metrics that are more aligned with the wisdom ingrained in the principles of interconnectedness?

In conclusion, the narrative of resurrection—of life blooming anew from the ashes—is a compelling catalyst for applying wisdom to failing systems. From acknowledging the inevitability of cycles to respecting the intricate web of life, these lessons from ancient spiritual wisdom provide a blueprint for a more responsible and enlightened approach to technology and system development. As much as the prospect of resurrection is an inspiring message of hope, it's also a call to action—a gentle nudging towards engaging with technology as an extension of our collective wisdom. A rebirth of sorts, from technology as a mere tool, to technology as a conscious entity—grounded in the wisdom of the ages, illuminating our digital future.

Chapter 11. The Second Coming: Anticipating the Future of IoT and Spirituality

In a world delicately draped between technological advancements and timeless spirituality, it's necessary to pause, ponder and anticipate what lies ahead in this incipient amalgamation. One can't help but turn to 'The Second Coming,' a notion deeply rooted in Christian theology. This anticipatory event is akin to forecasting the future of the Internet of Things (IoT) and spirituality – both carry a sense of hope, future impact, and transformation.

11.1. Anticipating IoT's Evolution

The Internet of Things (IoT) is not merely a succession of devices connected to the Internet. Its essence lies in a world of interconnections, where objects equipped with sensors and processing ability communicate with each other, with humans, and with wider systems. In many ways, this mirrors the interconnectedness propagated by Jesus Christ — the concept of unity amongst humanity and with the divine.

But what does the future hold for IoT? Beyond the smart refrigerators and voice-controlled lighting systems, there is a much deeper level of integration and sophistication yet to be unfurled. Experts predict a rise in city-wide systems propelled by IoT, where waste management, traffic control, and public safety aren't standalone units but part of a unified smart system. The benevolence of this connectedness would make urban living more efficient and sustainable, reminding us of Jesus' teachings about stewardship of resources.

However, just as the concept of the Second Coming inspires hope but also carries a warning, the future of IoT isn't devoid of pitfalls. Amid the advantages, threats of security breaches, privacy invasion, and over-reliance on AI raise concerns. This necessitates the integration of ethics and a sense of shared responsibility into our technological march forward, a principle Jesus preached extensively in his parables.

11.2. Synergy of Spirituality and Technology

The intersect of spirituality and technology might seem unfamiliar at first. However, with closer scrutiny, one notices how spirituality and technology can, surprisingly, complement and enhance each other. In essence, the teachings of Jesus Christ promote love, compassion, responsibility, and conscientious action — qualities vital to the development and use of IoT. What could be more 'connected' than the empathy and understanding that comes from accepting a universal force that unifies us all?

From the inception of the Internet age, it is observed that technology has increasingly become a vessel for spiritual practice. Sacred texts are digitized for wider access, meditation and prayers apps are proliferating, even religious rituals can now be conducted virtually. It's a whole new era of digital spiritual communion, a transformation aided by technology.

The future could see IoT playing a larger role in our spiritual journeys. Virtual Reality (VR) and Augmented Reality (AR) can render immersive spiritual experiences; AI-powered robots might help teach and discuss religious texts, or perhaps smart wearables could remind us of prayer times or moral codes. Such fusion of the spiritual and technological can serve to deepen our spiritual consciousness, replacing religious isolation with a connected ecosystem of faith.

11.3. The Next Spiritual Revolution?

While thinking of revolution, we often envision disruptive change, but the word 'revolution' also hints at the cyclical nature of change. There's an interesting parallel here to the Second Coming, a cyclic event which in Christian belief promises renewal.

As we anticipate the evolution of IoT, might we be on the cusp of the next spiritual revolution? The combination of theology and technology is holding a mirror to the dichotomy of our world, allowing us to really reflect on the acceleration of our material advancement vis-à-vis spiritual growth.

The ever-evolving IoT could foster an era where technology supports, rather than impedes, our spirituality. This vision is not utopian but possible when technology is ethically grounded and spiritually directed. The intersectionality might elucidate a path of spiritual progression parallel to technological sophistication.

11.4. Navigating the Path Ahead

While the future of IoT and spirituality is speculative, the understanding that we're evolving towards a more holistic future is quite certain. However, navigating the inherent complexities of this evolution require due consideration. As we build technology with spirituality as its cornerstone, we must also recognize the potential pitfalls.

Firstly, balancing privacy with personalization would be a continual challenge. While smart devices could offer personalized spiritual experiences, they could also potentially infringe on intimate spaces.

Secondly, it is important not to entirely substitute human interaction with technological interfaces in our spiritual journeys. The human touch often brings subtle nuances that a machine cannot replicate.

We must tread the delicate balance between maximizing the benefits of technology and preserving the raw, organic essence of spiritual communion.

Lastly, we must ask ourselves — how do we ensure this interplay of technology and spirituality catalyzes unity and not division? We must establish a critical dialogue around developing inclusive technologies that respect diverse beliefs and practices.

The future of IoT and spirituality is uncharted yet promising. It's a journey we're embarking on collectively, navigating through persistent transformations. This endeavor doesn't merely echo the practical implications of the 'Second Coming,' it also underscores the essence of the doctrine — a hope of reinvention and the promise of a new beginning. Just as 'The Second Coming' breathes new life into Christian theology, so might technology invigorate our spiritual experiences, making them not just personal, but globally and universally connected.

www.ingramcontent.com/pod-product-compliance
Lightning Source LLC
Chambersburg PA
CBHW071016260726
48661CB00007B/2986